Pebble®

Families

Grandfathers

Revised and Updated

by Lola M. Schaefer

Consulting Editor: Gail Saunders-Smith, PhD

Capstone press®
Mankato, Minnesota

T0052530

Pebble Books are published by Capstone Press,
1710 Roe Crest Drive, North Mankato, Minnesota 56003.
www.capstonepress.com

Copyright © 2008 by Capstone Press, a Capstone Publishers company.
All rights reserved. No part of this publication may be reproduced in whole or in part, or stored in a retrieval system, or transmitted in any form or by any means, electronic, mechanical, photocopying, recording, or otherwise, without written permission of the publisher.
For information regarding permission, write to Capstone Press,
1710 Roe Crest Drive, North Mankato, Minnesota 56003.

Library of Congress Cataloging-in-Publication Data
Schaefer, Lola M., 1950–
Grandfathers/by Lola M. Schaefer. — Rev. and updated.
p. cm. — (Pebble books. Families)
Includes bibliographical references and index.
Summary: "Simple text and photographs present grandfathers and how they interact with their families" — Provided by publisher.
ISBN-13: 978-1-4296-1225-8 (hardcover)
ISBN-10: 1-4296-1225-8 (hardcover)
ISBN-13: 978-1-4296-1754-3 (softcover)
ISBN-10: 1-4296-1754-3 (softcover)
1. Grandfathers — Juvenile literature. 2. Grandparent and child — Juvenile literature. I. Title. II. Series.
HQ759.9.S34 2008
306.874'5 — dc22 2007027095

Note to Parents and Teachers

The Families set supports national social studies standards related to identifying family members and their roles in the family. This book describes and illustrates grandfathers. The images support early readers in understanding the text. The repetition of words and phrases helps early readers learn new words. This book also introduces early readers to subject-specific vocabulary words, which are defined in the glossary section. Early readers may need some assistance to read some words and to use the Table of Contents, Glossary, Read More, Internet Sites, and Index sections of the book.

Printed in the United States 4964

Table of Contents

Grandfathers 5
Busy Grandfathers 9
At Play 15

Glossary 22
Read More 23
Internet Sites. 23
Index 24

Grandfathers

Grandfathers are fathers of mothers and fathers.

Grandfathers
have grandchildren.

Busy Grandfathers

Grandfathers are busy.
Grandpa Fred
owns a bakery.

114

Grandpa George
builds bird houses.

Grandpa Les
goes for walks.

At Play

Grandfathers have fun.
Grandpa Lee
plays catch.

Grandpa Bill

comes to tea parties.

Today is

Grandpa Ed reads stories.

Grandfathers love
their grandchildren.

Glossary

bakery — a store or building where bread, cake, cookies, and other foods are baked in ovens

father — a male parent; your dad's father is your grandfather.

grandchildren — the children of a grandfather's son or daughter

mother — a female parent; your mom's father is your grandfather.

own — to have something that belongs to you; people who own businesses are in charge of that business.

Read More

Parr, Todd. *The Grandpa Book.* New York: Little, Brown, 2006.

Robertson, J. Jean. *Meet My Grandparents.* Vero Beach, Fla.: Rourke, 2007.

Internet Sites

FactHound offers a safe, fun way to find Internet sites related to this book. All of the sites on FactHound have been researched by our staff.

Here's how:

1. Visit *www.facthound.com*
2. Choose your grade level.
3. Type in this book ID **1429612258** for age-appropriate sites. You may also browse subjects by clicking on letters, or by clicking on pictures and words.
4. Click on the **Fetch It** button.

FactHound will fetch the best sites for you!

Index

bakery, 9
building things, 11
fathers, 5
grandchildren, 7, 21
Grandpa Bill, 17
Grandpa Ed, 19
Grandpa Fred, 9
Grandpa George, 11
Grandpa Lee, 15
Grandpa Les, 13
mothers, 5
reading stories, 19
tea parties, 17
walking, 13

Word Count: 49
Grade 1
Early-Intervention Level: 10

Editorial Credits
Sarah L. Schuette, revised edition editor; Kim Brown, revised edition designer

Photo Credits
Capstone Press, cover; Karon Dubke, interiors